Grey Owl

VICKY SHIPTON

Level 3

Series Editors: Andy Hopkins and Jocelyn Potter

ESL CENTER

Pearson Education Limited

Edinburgh Gate, Harlow,
Essex CM20 2JE, England
and Associated Companies throughout the world.

ISBN: 978-1-4058-8185-2

First published by Penguin Books 2003
This edition first published 2008

3 5 7 9 10 8 6 4 2

Typeset by Graphicraft Ltd, Hong Kong
Set in 11/14pt Bembo
Printed in China
SWTC/02

Published by Pearson Education Ltd in association with
Penguin Books Ltd, both companies being subsidiaries of Pearson Plc

Acknowledgements

Archives of Ontario: pp 2 (C 273-1-0-44-1), 23 (C 273-1-0-17-16) and 27 (C 273-1-0-36-26);
Corbis: pp 4 and 40;
Glenbow Archives: pp 18, 21, 25, 33, 35 and 37.

For a complete list of the titles available in the Penguin Readers series please write to your local
Pearson Longman office or to: Penguin Readers Marketing Department, Pearson Education,
Edinburgh Gate, Harlow, Essex CM20 2JE, England.

Contents

Introduction

He understood what was happening in Canada. More and more people were killing beavers. The animal was in terrible danger. But he knew how important this animal was to the Canadian forest and its people. In a way, the beaver was the Canadian forest. And so he found a new purpose in life. He decided to fight for the beaver . . .

Grey Owl loved the forests of Canada and their many animals. He was sad and angry because every year more trees were cut down. Every year more animals were killed. But could one man save the land that he loved? How could he send this message to the world? It was a difficult job. But Grey Owl knew that he must not fail. It was too important.

Today, more and more people understand how important this message is. But seventy years ago, Grey Owl's thoughts and ideas were new and surprising to many people.

This book tells the story of Grey Owl and his message. He was a man who tried to change the world. But the book also tells the strange story of the man behind the message. Grey Owl was a man with a big secret. Few people knew the real person. Who was he? What was he hiding? What is the true story of Grey Owl?

Vicky Shipton is from Michigan, in the United States. She lived in Wisconsin in the northern United States for a long time, and she enjoyed walking in the woods near her home. She now lives in Cambridge, England, with her husband and two daughters.

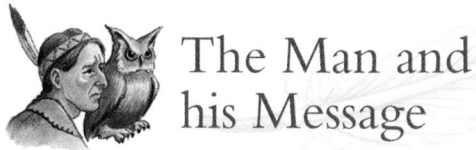

The Man and his Message

> "Remember. You belong to Nature,
> not it to you." GREY OWL

Many people could not get into the theater because it was full. Inside, the crowd waited without a sound. They were there to listen to one man. At last, the speaker was introduced. The theater was dark; there was one bright light on the stage. And then he was there—Grey Owl, the most famous North American Indian in the world.

He was tall and his dark face was serious. His clothes were made from animal skins. His long, black hair was tied back. In it, he wore one tall feather.

The year was 1937 and the theater was in London. To the people of that city, Grey Owl did not seem real. He spoke about the land and the animals of his home, Canada. He described his life in those great forests, rivers, and lakes. He even showed a film of the land and of his pet beavers playing.

For many people in the audience, these pictures were wonderful. Life in Britain was hard at the time; it was hard in much of the world. A lot of people did not have jobs. In the opinion of many, war in Europe was coming soon. There was already war in Spain, and people read about Hitler and Mussolini with fear in their hearts. But in this difficult time, Grey Owl showed a different world—a better world.

In Grey Owl's world people did *not* live in dirty, crowded cities. They did not have boring jobs and they did not worry about world war. Grey Owl's description of Canada's wild forests was a dream for many people.

Grey Owl was the most famous North American Indian in the world.

It was important for them to see a man like this. Most people only knew stories about North American Indians. The writers of these books often knew nothing about their subjects' real lives. In these stories, the Indians were often wild "savages." The ways of the "white man" were better. But Grey Owl was clearly an intelligent man. He spoke beautifully about his people and their way of life. In fact, he was angry about the white man's way of life in North America. It was destroying his beautiful country.

Not From India

The native people of North America were first called Indians because of a mistake. Christopher Columbus was sailing for India, but he reached America. People described the native people of this land as "Red Indians" because of the color of their skin. One newspaper wrote about Grey Owl, "There never came a redder Red Indian to Britain."

Today, many native peoples in Canada and the United States like to use the name Native Americans. Others still use the name Indians or American Indians. Nobody says "Red Indian" today.

Grey Owl's message to the world was clear. In his country, Indians only killed enough animals for food and clothes. They only cut down enough trees for their homes and their fires. They did not destroy the natural world. They loved it and lived with it. In Grey Owl's opinion, everybody in the world should act in this way.

Today, a lot of people agree with Grey Owl's message. They know that many animals are in danger in the modern world. We should protect them. We should not cut down all of our forests. More and more people think that we must look after the Earth. But seventy years ago, this opinion was not so popular. Grey Owl

Canada's beautiful lakes and forests were Grey Owl's home.

was one of the first people in the world to speak about these things. He said something new and important.

For years in the 1930s, Grey Owl traveled and spoke to large audiences. He was famous around the world. His trip in 1937 was his second tour of Britain as a speaker. He even met the King and Queen in Buckingham Palace. His message was also on every page of his books.

But what did people know about this man? His books described his parents in this way: His father was from Scotland. His mother was an Apache Indian from New Mexico, in the South West of the United States. He spent part of his early life in Mexico.

It was an exciting story, but the real story of Grey Owl was more interesting than this. "Grey Owl" had a secret.

# The Secret Uncovered

Grey Owl looked and acted like an Indian. But there were questions about him. How could he write English so well? Did another person write his books for him? Then people heard him speak. Grey Owl clearly wrote the books—his English was excellent. But how did he learn to speak the language so well?

Grey Owl continued to speak to crowds in Britain and North America. On March 29, 1938, he gave his last talk. It was in Regina, Canada. Then he went back to his home. He was very tired after all this travel and hard work.

He arrived home on April 7. Three days later, he called for help. He was not feeling well. He was taken to hospital quickly, but he died a few days later. Nobody knows the reason for his death. Was it too much hard work and travel? Or was he tired of living with a secret for so long?

After he died, there was a story in a small Canadian newspaper, the North Bay *Nugget*. Grey Owl had *no* Indian blood at all. His real name was Archibald (or Archie) Belaney. He was born in Hastings, England, in 1888. His mother Kittie Belaney and father George Belaney were both British. He grew up in a town in the south of England. He went to a good school.

Of course, some people in Canada already knew Archie Belaney's secret. They knew him *before* he was Grey Owl. In the rest of the world, people could not believe this news. But the North Bay *Nugget* could prove its story. It was true—Grey Owl, the most famous Indian in the world, was not an American Indian!

How could this happen? What was so different about this young British boy? How did he become the famous Indian called Grey Owl?

George Belaney wanted to make money, but he did not want to work hard. He tried to find success in the United States, but his business there failed.

The trees are dying. What will we do, George?

We'll go back to England.

Don't worry, Kittie. My mother will give us money.

In England, Kittie had a baby.

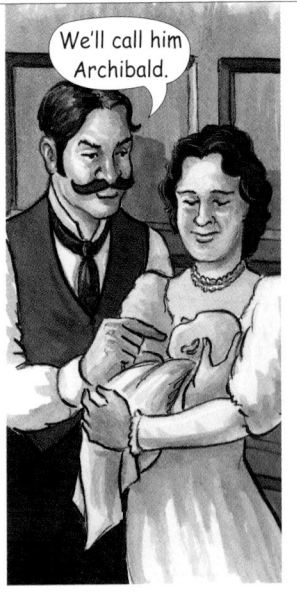

We'll call him Archibald.

George had a new idea.

Mother, I can succeed in North America. I know it!

Go, George. But Kittie and Archie must stay here.

Young Archie never saw his father again.

One day ...

Dear Kittie, please send money. Don't tell Mother. Your husband, George.

You are sending money to George! You must leave here, Kittie. Archibald will stay here.

Archie's aunts, Ada and Carrie, looked after him.

Archibald will be a good man.

Years passed.

Archie did not have many friends.

He was interested in other things.

I am an Indian!

I'm an owl!

Hoot!

Hoot!

Archie loved animals.

Great!

I found it in the woods.

You must take it upstairs!

I hate school! I want to leave.

Then you can work in an office. My friend has a job for you.

But ...

This is boring!

One day, some wood near the building blows up...

One person probably knew why it happened.

I'm going to Canada. I want to live in the woods.

Don't be like your father, Archie.

Good luck, Archie!

"Real" Indians

In March, 1906, Archie stepped onto a ship in Liverpool. He was seventeen years old. On April 6, he reached Halifax, Canada. He needed money and so he went first to the big city of Toronto. He worked for a few months as a shop assistant. But this was not what he wanted to do. He could work in a shop in England.

Archie decided to travel north. He took the train and got off at Témiscaming. At last, he was in the land of his dreams! He was lucky. He met a man called Bill Guppy. He stayed with Bill and his family that winter. Like Archie, Bill loved the country. The older man taught Archie to trap animals, throw knives, and walk across the deep snow.

Bill told Archie about Lake Temagami. It was a large lake with thousands of islands. The Canadian government protected this area and there were hotels for tourists. Bill worked as a guide there. He took tourists to hunt and fish. Bill helped Archie to get a job there also. The young man could not be a guide yet, but he did small jobs around the hotel.

In the middle of Lake Temagami was an island called Bear Island. This was the home of Ojibwa Indians. Of course, Archie wanted to know the Indians. He often traveled to the island in his canoe. He met two of the more important Indians—Michel Mathias and Ned White Bear—and they soon became his friends. They began to teach him their way of life. They helped him to understand the Indians' idea of nature.

Archie always carried a small black notebook with him. He started to write down Ojibwa words. He also began to wear some Indian clothes. The dreams of the young boy from Hastings were becoming real.

The Ojibwa

The Ojibwa tribe was the largest tribe of Indians north of Mexico. Three tribes around the Great Lakes and in Southern Canada joined together—the Ojibwa, Ottawa, and Potawatomi tribes. They formed one big tribe called the Three Fires.

Ojibwa Indians usually lived in homes made from trees. The women grew plants and the men hunted for animals and fished. When the animals moved to a different area, the Ojibwa moved, too. The Ojibwa were excellent at hunting, trapping, and fishing, so Archie had good teachers.

The Ojibwa also helped Archie to understand American Indians' ideas about life and nature. In their world, all the things in the forest—animals, trees, plants, and rocks—had souls, like people did. For this reason, American Indians only took what they needed from the forest.

When white Europeans came to North America, the Indians' way of life changed. The Indian "savages" were pushed from place to place. In 1885, the Canadian government made a new law. Indians could only live in some special areas. More laws made these areas smaller and smaller. But the Indians had to move with the animals. They could not always stay in one place. Life became very difficult for them.

When Archie discovered this, he became angry. The "white man" did not understand this land or this life. Years later, he fought hard to help all of the country's native people.

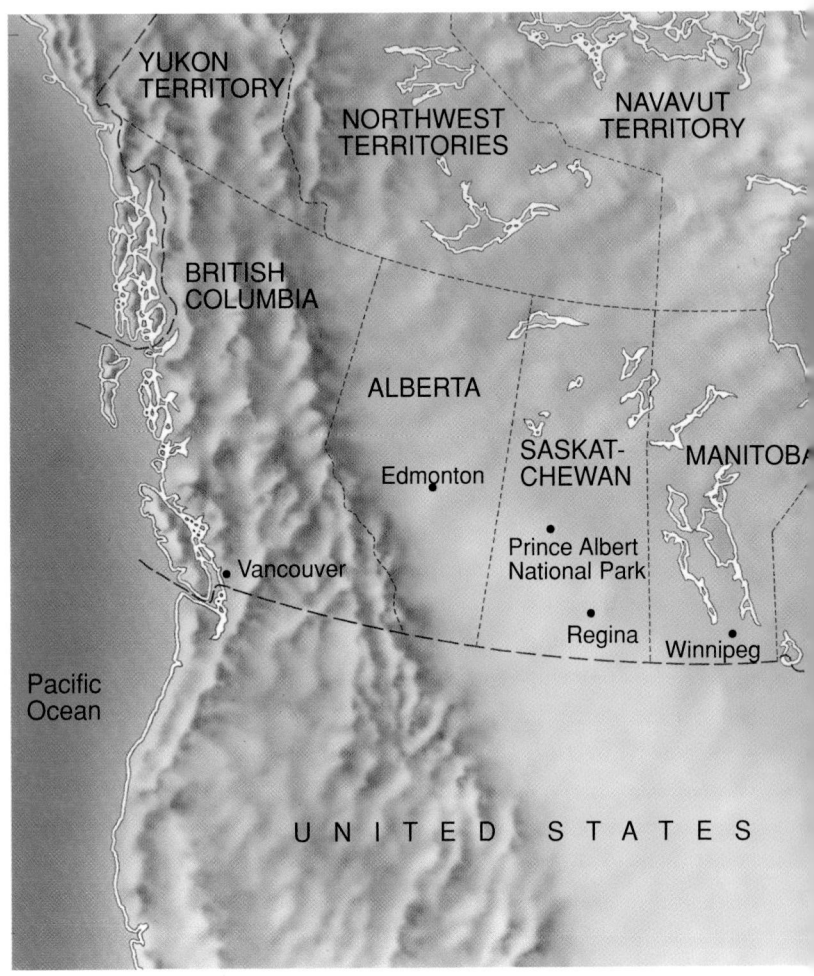

Canada

Canada is a very big country—the second biggest in the world. Even today, most of its population lives in the south of the country, near the United States. Much of the country is wild. It is home to many animals. The winters are very hard, with lots of snow and freezing temperatures.

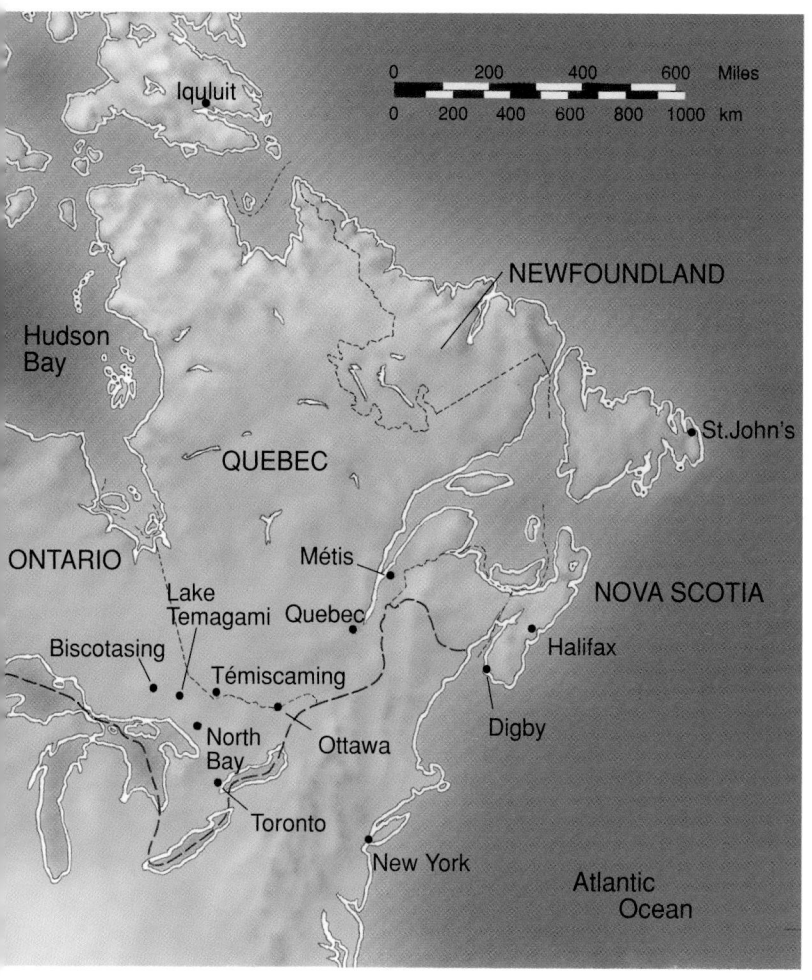

Europeans started to arrive in Canada in the 1600s. French people came first, and French is the first language of many Canadians today. But Britain ruled the country after 1763. British rule ended in 1931.

This map shows some of the places that Archie Belaney visited. As you read the rest of the book, look back at the map. You can see how far Archie traveled.

# First Marriage

Near the end of 1907, Archie went back to England. Some people believe that he needed more money. But he also went because his grandmother was very sick. In England, Archie dressed and looked more like an Indian. He only stayed for three unhappy months, and his mind was far away in the Canadian forests for all that time.

Back in Canada, Archie returned to his old job at Lake Temagami—and to the Ojibwa tribe on Bear Island. More and more, he seemed to try to forget his old life. He became friendly with a young Ojibwa woman. She worked in the kitchen at the hotel, and her name was Angele Egwuna. She did not speak English, but she and Archie became good friends. With Angele's help, he became closer to the Ojibwa people.

When Archie's old friend Bill Guppy saw him in 1908, the trapper was surprised. He remembered a friendly young man from England. Now Archie looked and acted like an Indian. His clothes, his hair, and even his walk were different.

On August 23, 1910, Archie married Angele Egwuna. They started life together in a tent on Bear Island. Angele still spoke almost no English, so she taught Archie her language. Sometimes he laughed and said to her, "I'll make a white woman of you!" Angele replied, "I'll make an Indian of you!"

In fact, Archie spent all his time now in the company of Indians. He was very proud of his Indian ways. He loved to hear the tribe's stories. Angele's uncle called Archie "Little Owl" because he watched everything carefully. He tried to learn it all.

Archie did learn a lot from Angele and her people. Years later, Grey Owl described young Indians in his book *Sajo and the*

Beaver People. The book tells how they learn about plants and trees. They learn the ways of animals. They learn the calls of the birds and animals in the forests. Archie often saw beavers on the island. In fact, Angele's family lived next to a beaver lodge. The beavers were friendly. Sometimes they came right up to the Indians.

Grey Owl later added some new facts to the story of his time with the Ojibwa. In his memory, the tribe welcomed him with a big party. They danced and sang and made owl noises. But none of the Ojibwa remembered this party!

Archie was happy with Angele at first, but he was also an angry man. He loved to fight with white men in the area. Archie began to make trouble in town. He did not know it, but he was acting more and more like his father.

Then Angele had a baby. As he held his new daughter, Agnes, Archie was afraid. Archie never knew his father or mother. He did not know what to do with the baby. Three months after Agnes was born, Archie left Bear Island.

He left the Indian way of life, too. In one letter, he described all the bad things about Indian life—it was not "like the books." At the time, Archie was trapping with three other white men. He sent money back to Angele and the baby, but he never wrote to them.

Archie's next job was as a fire ranger for a Canadian park, watching the forests for fires. He moved around a lot, but he did not go back to Angele or Agnes for a long, long time.

# Wild Days

In the summer of 1912, Archie went to Biscotasing. (The town is usually just called "Bisco.") His dark hair was long and straight now. His skin was dark from the sun. To the people in Bisco, Archie looked half-Indian and half-white.

Around this time, Archie started telling stories about his past. His mother was an Apache Indian and his father was from Scotland. He was born in Mexico and grew up in the American South West. He told one man that his father was a "Texan Ranger." He and his family traveled with Buffalo Bill's Wild West Show. He went to school in England while the show toured in Europe. Of course, these were all lies, but Archie told them for years. Sometimes he added to them. For example, his father was killed. Archie shot his father's killer and ran away to Canada.

Archie looked half-Indian and half-white.

Archie was still married to Angele, but he met another woman in Bisco. Marie Girard was a Métis woman. (The Métis were half-Ojibwa and half-French.) She agreed to go trapping with him that winter. Archie was lucky to have Marie with him. He was not a very good trapper. He sometimes forgot where his traps were. Marie helped him a lot, and they had a successful trapping season. Archie had another job, too, as a ranger. He had to protect the forest in the area. (Many people were looking for silver and gold near Bisco.)

Archie continued to watch everything around him and to make notes in his book. "Do you think that I can write?" he asked a friend, sitting at a fire one night. In fact, Archie wrote all the time, but he really wanted to write books.

But there was another side to Archie in Bisco. He still had time for trouble. He shouted at people in the street. He even threw knives at trains. Once, after his return from a trip into the woods, Archie destroyed part of an office. The police were looking for him, and Marie and Archie had to hide in the woods.

Archie left Marie that winter. No one knows exactly why. She was carrying a baby. Did Archie run because of this? Some old friends have said that Archie did not know about the child. We can't know, but one thing is sure. He never saw Marie again.

It was a year after the start of the First World War, and many Canadians wanted to fight for Britain. Archie traveled for four months, going more than 1,500 kilometers. He went to Digby, Nova Scotia, and he joined the Canadian Army on May 6, 1915. He gave his real name, Archie Belaney, but he told many lies, too. He was born in Toronto. He fought in a war in Mexico. He did not tell the army about his wife, Angele, or his child.

In June, Archie sailed for England as a soldier. When he arrived, he left the army for two weeks. He wanted to visit his two aunts in Hastings. He did not tell the army what he was doing. Archie was in trouble again.

War and Wives

Archie was a good soldier. After all his time in the Canadian forests, he was very good at shooting. He could sit quietly for hours and watch for enemies. One soldier remembers thinking that Archie was Indian or half-Indian. Nobody could hide from enemy soldiers as well as Archie.

The war was terrible. Tens of thousands of men died on both sides. In the fields of Belgium, Archie saw death everywhere. One night he put his coat on a tree. In the morning, he saw that it was not a tree. It was the arm of a dead soldier.

In January, 1916, Archie was shot in the hand. He went to a hospital for a few weeks to get better. But he was soon hurt again. This time he was shot in the foot. He lost a toe and part of his foot. Archie's war ended. He was sent back to England.

Years later, Grey Owl spoke about the First World War. The war taught us a terrible lesson about the modern world, he said. It was more savage than any native people. Maybe he did believe this when he was older. But immediately after the war, Archie seemed to want the modern world again.

He spent a long time in hospitals in England. He even stayed in a hospital in his home town, Hastings. His aunts visited him, but Archie was very lonely. His aunts had an idea. He should call his old school friend, Ivy Holmes.

Archie was an unusual man, but Ivy's life was different, too. She was twenty-six and she worked as a dancer. Before the war, she traveled around Europe. Archie seemed very exciting to her. She loved the stories that he told her. Ivy helped him to get better after his terrible time in the war. The two became very close.

On February 10, 1917, Archie and Ivy were married at a beautiful church in a small town near Hastings. Of course, Ivy did not know that Archie was still married to Angele in Canada! What was Archie thinking? Was he trying to forget his life as an Indian? As usual with Archie Belaney, the answer is a mystery.

In March, 1917, Archie's foot was much better and he could walk again. He told Ivy his hopes. He wanted them to go back to Canada—to Bisco! Marie lived there, and Archie's wife Angele lived only 100 kilometers away. Again, we can't imagine what was in Archie's mind. But Ivy was excited at the idea of living in the Canadian forests. She agreed to go.

Archie traveled first, leaving on September 19, 1917. He wanted his new wife to come and meet him later. But terrible news was waiting for Archie back in Canada.

Ivy worked as a dancer.

 # A Father for Archie

While Archie was at war, thousands of kilometers away in Bisco Marie had her baby. Johnny Jero was born on September 16, 1915. Sadly, Marie died a few weeks later. Many people in Bisco were very angry with Archie because he left Marie.

Archie could not bring Ivy to Bisco now, but he was afraid to tell her why. He continued to write to her for almost a year. Finally, he told her about Angele, his first wife. Ivy immediately ended their "marriage" and she never spoke to Archie again. His aunts were very angry with him, too. They did not know anything about Angele until then.

Back in Bisco, Archie worked as a trapper and a fire ranger again. He was not happy. His foot hurt and he was lonely. But he seemed to enjoy being the bad man in town again. Then he met an Indian family that became an important part of his life.

For two or three summers he lived with the Espaniel family. Alex Espaniel was like a father to Archie—his only "father" ever. Jim and Jane, two of Alex's children, became good friends with Archie.

Alex was very kind. He often looked after people who needed help. He took Archie trapping. He taught the younger man many Ojibwa ways. He showed him how to look after beavers.

Archie studied hard. He wrote everything in a notebook. He drew pictures and wrote stories. He tried hard to look like an Indian again. The short hair of the war years was gone. Archie even colored his hair and skin darker. He tried to walk and stand like an Indian. He looked in the mirror for hours, trying to "look Indian."

Archie still had his wild side, too. One time, he blew up a beaver lodge in the forest. Alex was very angry about this. He almost told Archie to leave. Why was Archie still looking for trouble in this way? Like his father, Archie never seemed happy. He was always looking for something more in his life, but he did not know what.

Even Alex—Archie's new "father"—could not keep Archie out of trouble. In the end, Archie did have to leave the Espaniels. He was in trouble with the Bisco police again. It was time for him to move away.

In the summer of 1925, he went back to Lake Temagami and worked as a guide. He took tourists into the forests to look for animals. He also took them in his canoe. He sometimes stayed with Angele, his first wife, and their daughter Agnes. Agnes said of her father, "He was not interested in white people."

Angele still loved Archie. But Archie still did not enjoy family life. He left again in the fall of 1925. The next spring, Angele had another daughter, Flora. But she never saw Archie again.

Alex Espaniel was like a father to Archie.

# True Love

Archie never had trouble meeting women. Many of them wanted to know more about the mysterious Indian. They came to him. But one day everything changed. It was late summer, 1925, and Archie was in his canoe. Then he saw her—Gertrude Bernard. She was sitting by the lake and she was reading a book. She was a nineteen-year-old Iroquois Indian and she was beautiful. Archie knew immediately that he wanted her.

Gertrude was from the city, but she wanted to see more of the woods. So she was working in a restaurant on Lake Temagami. Her friends did not call her "Gertrude;" they called her "Pony." It was a good name for her—she was strong and fast, and she loved nature.

Gertrude was an intelligent woman who stopped going to school at a young age. When Archie saw her, she was planning to leave Lake Temagami soon. A rich family offered to pay for her to go to a church school in Toronto.

Archie knew that he must talk to her. He walked up to her and said the first thing in his head: "Do you have any potatoes?" But it worked and they met a few times in the next few weeks. Then Gertrude went home to Mattawa.

But that did not stop Archie. He wrote a lot of letters to her. One of them was almost 100 pages long! He wanted her to return to the woods. Pony was interested in the old Indian ways. She wanted an exciting life. But Archie's letters did not change her mind. In the end, he visited her. Pony agreed to come to the woods for a short visit before school started.

Archie was ready. He and his friends even built a cabin for Pony. The two of them went trapping. She did not like to see the animals die, but she loved life in the woods. And she was starting to love Archie, too.

Gertrude did not go to school in Toronto. She stayed with Archie and learned about the old ways of life in the woods. They lived and worked together. They were a great team. Archie told her stories of the old ways. He even gave her an Indian name—Anahareo. This was a happy time for Archie. He wrote about it in a letter to his aunts. His letter was full of his love for the forests.

Archie even started to tell Anahareo about his life. He told her many of his secrets. He told her about his wives and children. To Anahareo, these stories made Archie more interesting and exciting. But he could not tell her his biggest secret. She knew nothing about Archie's early years. She did not know that he had no Indian blood.

Archie and Anahareo outside their cabin.

A New Life

As Archie taught Anahareo about life in the woods, he continued to do the same kinds of jobs as before. Often he worked for the Canadian Parks Service. In the summer of 1925 he was a fire ranger again. In the winter, he protected forest animals from people who hunted without permission.

In the winter of 1926–27, Anahareo asked to go trapping with Archie. She went, but she hated it. She hated to see the animals dying and in pain. She wanted Archie to stop.

Slowly, Archie changed his mind about trapping also. He understood what was happening in Canada. More and more people were killing beavers. The animal was in terrible danger. But he knew how important this animal was to the Canadian forest and its people. In a way, the beaver *was* the Canadian forest. And so he found a new purpose in life. Archie decided to fight for the beaver and help this beautiful animal.

Around this time, Archie heard a voice from his past. He received a letter from his mother, Kittie. She got his address from the Canadian government. Archie wrote to her, telling her about his life in the Canadian woods. The description in his letter was wonderful, and Kittie sent it to an important British magazine, *Country Life.* They loved it, also. They asked Archie to write more for them. They even wanted him to write a book. At last, after years of writing everything in his black notebook, Archie was becoming a real writer.

A New Name

When they were reading about life in the forest, people wanted to read the words of a real Indian. Archie was sure about this. So, when he wrote to *Country Life* in November, 1929, he signed his name "Grey Owl" for the first time. (Before that, he tried the name "White Owl.") In his words, he was an "Indian writer." Now Archie could not turn back from his life of lies. The young boy from Hastings made owl noises. The man was now the Indian Grey Owl.

 # Life with the Beavers

Archie—or Grey Owl—wrote about all of the things that were important to him. One of these was the beaver. In the spring of 1928, he found two kits.* Their mother was dead and they could not live without her. Archie took them home to live with him and Anahareo.

They named the two beavers McGinnis and McGinty because Irish workers on the North American trains had names like these. Archie enjoyed studying the beavers and their way of life. He and Anahareo loved them. The animals were almost like their children.

They moved with the beavers many times. They wanted McGinnis and McGinty to find a family of wild beavers. But then a terrible thing happened. The two beavers disappeared. At last, a sad Archie realized that the beavers were dead. A trapper probably caught them.

An Indian friend, Dave White Stone, found two more beaver kits alone in the woods. He took them to Archie and Anahareo. One of the beavers died, but the other kit lived. It soon had a name—Jelly Roll.

Jelly Roll and Archie became good friends. Archie did not like to be with people when he was writing—not even Anahareo. But Jelly Roll was always there in the cabin with him. Archie's bed was very low because Jelly Roll liked to be able to see him!

Archie moved near the vacation town of Métis in the summer of 1929. Many people in this town did not know the woods very

* kits: young beavers

well. They paid ten cents to see Jelly Roll. Someone asked Archie to give a talk at the local hotel about his life. Archie was nervous, but he said yes. The audience loved his talk and he earned $700. Newspapers in the area began to write about Grey Owl. They called him "the beaver man."

Someone in the government heard about the Indian "beaver man." The government wanted more tourists to visit Canadian parks. So in June, 1930, the Canadian Parks Service came and made a film of Grey Owl and Jelly Roll. The film was shown all over the country. It was very popular. People loved to watch the little beaver playing. It enjoyed moving things around. When it was hungry, it liked to bite wooden things in the cabin. At first, Archie tried to stop it, but then he changed his mind. He could always get new things!

Later that year, Archie found another beaver—Rawhide. Rawhide and Jelly Roll were happy together. But in the winter of 1930–31, the two beavers built a home on the lake and then they disappeared. Were they dead? Archie discovered the answer in spring. The beavers came out with their four new kits— Wakanee, Wakanoo, Buckshot, and Silver Bells. Archie knew now that Jelly Roll was a female!

In 1931, the Canadian Parks Service asked Grey Owl to move to a big new park called the Prince Albert National Park. They built a cabin for him and Anahareo there. It was next to the lake where the beavers lived. It was called Beaver Lodge. Grey Owl had to watch the beavers and write about them. He showed the beavers and other animals to visitors. He told his stories. It was a perfect job for him.

Grey Owl started to travel more and more to give talks. But he always returned to Beaver Lodge. He wrote all of his books there, and he stayed there until his death in 1938.

Beavers

Beavers are large animals that always live near water. They can grow to about one meter long. Their short front legs are very strong. They have big back feet for swimming. Beavers also have big, flat tails. Their tail is very important. It helps them to swim. It also helps them to stand up when they are eating. They hit the water with it to send messages to other beavers.

The best-known part of the beaver is probably its big front teeth. These never stop growing. Beavers use their strong teeth to bite through trees. The teeth look quite strange—they are bright orange!

Beavers use trees for many purposes. They eat them. They also build their homes with them. A beaver's home is called a lodge.

Beavers live in a lodge until there is no more wood around it. Then they move and build a new home. In this way, beavers can change forests. They cut down trees and they can stop rivers.

The beaver must swim under the water to get into a lodge.

The beaver was always very important to American Indians in the north. When beavers moved, the Indians usually followed. They killed the animal for its meat, and they made clothes from its fur. Because the animals spend a lot of time in cold water, beavers have very thick fur.

When Europeans came to North America, they wanted the beaver for this beautiful, thick fur. Many people in cities wanted to wear fur coats. Trappers could sell beaver fur for a lot of money. They killed more and more beavers, until the animal was in great danger.

A Beaver's Lodge

A family of beavers usually lives in a lodge. Beavers have 2-4 kits every year. The babies stay until they are two years old. Then they leave to start new families.

The floor of the lodge is above the water.

Grey Owl's Books

Grey Owl finished his first book while he was living with the beavers. He was very serious about writing and he worked hard on the book. He wanted to call it *Vanishing Frontier*. In the book, he explained how to live with nature.

Grey Owl was not happy when *Country Life* changed the title of the book. They published it under the title *Men of the Last Frontier*. In Grey Owl's opinion, the book was not about men. It was about the natural world. He decided to offer his next book to a different publishing company. A small Canadian company published his next book. Grey Owl was lucky to find this company. The owner, Lovat Dickson, had big plans for Grey Owl. He wanted to make him a star. In Dickson's opinion, Grey Owl should travel and talk to people as much as possible.

Grey Owl agreed because he wanted to explain his message about nature to as many people as possible. But he was also very happy to be famous. Maybe this was why, years before, he was always looking for trouble in Bisco. He liked to be different. He liked people to notice him.

Grey Owl's second book, *Pilgrims of the Wild*, was published in 1934. It told the story of Grey Owl and Anahareo. The book explained why they stopped trapping. Anahareo was very important in the book and readers loved her. Grey Owl wanted her to speak on the tour also, but Anahareo refused. This was just one of the growing problems between them.

Grey Owl sits at his table in Beaver Lodge. He wrote all of his books here.

Grey Owl's third book was published in 1935. It was called *Sajo and the Beaver People*. Many children enjoyed this story about two beaver kits. In the story, an Indian finds the young beavers. He takes them home, and he and his children become their friends. Soon everyone in the town loves the two animals. In the end, they leave and join some wild beavers in the woods. Of course, the story was quite similar to Grey Owl's real life with beavers.

Grey Owl continued to tour, and more and more people were buying his books. *Pilgrims of the Wild* sold more than 35,000 copies. When *Sajo* came out, it sold 1,000 copies every week at first!

Archie Belaney had what he always wanted. He was Grey Owl, the Indian writer. But this did not always make him happy. A lot of publishers wanted Grey Owl to write for them. He did not feel free. In one year, he said no to over thirty people.

Grey Owl's last book was *Tales of an Empty Cabin*. It was published in 1936. Again, its subject was nature, and Grey Owl's message was the same. People should love the natural world and not destroy it. In the beginning of the book, Grey Owl asks people to go to the woods and take off their hats and shoes. They should look at the forest and give thanks for everything around them.

One story in the book is called "The Tree." It tells the story of a tree that is 650 years old. Over the years, the tree watches all the living things of the forest around it. Then people arrive and everything changes. They throw trash next to the tree. They cut down all the other trees. Finally, they cut down the great tree also, and they build a road in its place. Then they drive on the road. And they say that the land is ugly.

All of Grey Owl's strongest feelings and fears about nature went into this sad story. It was later published alone as a book. For many people, it was the perfect story for Grey Owl's message to the world.

In Grey Owl's third book, Sajo and the Beaver People, *an Indian finds some beaver kits. He becomes their friend. The story is very similar to Grey Owl's real life.*

# On Stage

Grey Owl traveled and gave many talks in the 1930s. Because he wanted people to hear his important message, they were good shows. In his wonderful Indian clothes, he looked like a chief on stage. When he was in theaters, he also showed the film of Jelly Roll. Because this was so popular, the Parks Service decided to make a second film about Grey Owl and his beavers. The film-makers took the top off Grey Owl's cabin so they could film everything!

Another Goodbye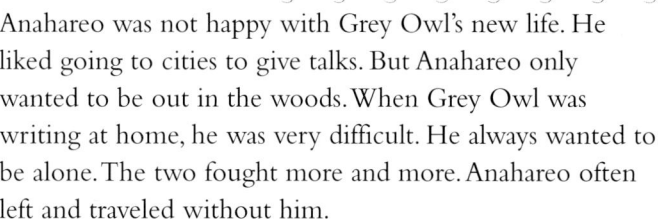

Anahareo was not happy with Grey Owl's new life. He liked going to cities to give talks. But Anahareo only wanted to be out in the woods. When Grey Owl was writing at home, he was very difficult. He always wanted to be alone. The two fought more and more. Anahareo often left and traveled without him.

She had a baby—Shirley Dawn—in 1932, but family life was becoming more difficult. Anahareo could not live with Grey Owl. She finally left him in 1936. Like so many people in Archie's life, she never saw him again.

His private life was unhappy, but Grey Owl was becoming more and more popular. His first British tour in 1935–36 was a big success. He spoke to thousands of people. In the busy cities, people loved to hear about the Canadian forest and its wild animals, its clean air, and its clear water. The newspapers loved him, too, and they wrote story after story about this great Indian. Grey Owl was a star.

Back home in Canada, Grey Owl talked often about the needs of Indians. They could not live their lives under the government's laws for the land. In his opinion, the government was not fair to the tribes. He wanted to help as much as possible. When one Indian chief came to Toronto, Grey Owl invited him to stay at his hotel. He also took him to meet important politicians.

During another tour of Canada, Grey Owl met a French–Canadian woman called Yvonne Perrier. In November, 1936, he asked Yvonne to marry him. Archie was marrying again! Yvonne started to help him with the long, hard work of his tours. At one place in November, he spoke to more than 1,700 people. Five hundred more people could not get in to see him.

Grey Owl was busier and busier. In 1937, he wanted to make two new films—one in the winter and one in the summer. His publishing company agreed to pay for the winter film. They finished the film in March, 1937. But Grey Owl did not look well in the film. He really needed to rest, but he refused to.

Archie and his new wife, Yvonne Perrier.

A Last Trip Home

Grey Owl went to the small town of North Bay, north of Toronto. A reporter from the local newspaper, the *Nugget,* was asking him questions. Suddenly the reporter said a name that Grey Owl knew very well—"Archie Belaney." The reporter knew Grey Owl's secret! He learned it when he spoke to Archie's first wife, Angele. Archie did not know what to do. He left the town quickly. He went back to Beaver Lodge and made his last film.

Archie waited and waited, but the newspaper did not print the story. The people at the North Bay *Nugget* liked Grey Owl. He was sending a good message to the world. They did not want to destroy him, and so they decided not to print the story. The newspaper only told the secret of Grey Owl after he died.

His secret was still safe, and Grey Owl went on his second tour of Britain later that year. Yvonne traveled with him. Again, the tour was a great success. To the people of Britain, Grey Owl was the voice of all American Indians. But for Archie, this trip was full of faces from the past.

In Oxford, an old woman came to his hotel. Yvonne did not know it, but this was Archie's mother, Kittie! Mother and son spoke for a long time. "I have only just begun my life," Archie told her seriously. Later, he sent her a ticket for his talk. When Grey Owl, the son of an Apache mother, spoke that night, his real mother—British, not Apache—was watching.

More of Archie's past was waiting for him. In December, he spoke in his home town, Hastings. It is not clear why, but Archie wanted to speak there. On the night of the talk, the sister of an old school friend was in the audience. She could not believe her

Grey Owl sent a good message to the world. Here, he feeds an adult beaver.

eyes. Later she told her brother, "That's Archie Belaney or I'll eat my hat!"

But for Archie the most important meeting came after the talk. He took Yvonne to see his two aunts, Carrie and Ada. Of course, Yvonne did not know who these old women really were.

The aunts were quite old now. What did they think when they saw Archie in his Indian clothes? And what thoughts went through Archie's mind when he looked at the old sitting room? The piano was still there. On the shelves there were copies of Grey Owl's four books. We can only guess what Archie and his aunts talked about that night. This was his last visit home.

After more tours of the United States and Canada, Grey Owl and Yvonne were very tired. Yvonne had to go to hospital. But Grey Owl was happy to be back at Beaver Lodge. This was his home now.

But the end was near. Archie seemed to know this. Not long before he died, he wrote, "I can never leave again." He wrote about the people who knew about his true past. "I have tried my best," wrote Grey Owl.

He died on April 13, 1938. Now the world could know his secret.

Maybe Archie Belaney was an Indian, in a way. In the words of American Indian writer N. Scott Momaday, "An Indian is an idea . . ."

The Memory of Grey Owl

After Archie died, the Prince Albert National Park did not look after his house. Maybe they wanted to forget the story of the Indian who was not an Indian. But, as the years passed, opinions slowly changed. Now more people remember what was good about Archie Belaney. The park built Beaver Lodge again. Today you can visit it and learn more about the man and his life.

But not many visitors will find the answers to all their questions. Who was Archie Belaney really? The man was a mystery. He loved the natural world and the native people of Canada, but he hurt everybody in his private life. He told lies for most of his years. Is it possible that part of him started to believe those lies? Did he like being a famous star, or was nature his only real love?

We can be sure of one thing—Archie Belaney lived a life full of lies, but Grey Owl's message was important and true. And that message is still true today. If we do not look after the natural world, we will lose it.

ACTIVITIES

Pages 1–4

Before you read

1 Look at the Word List at the back of the book. Use some of the words to complete these sentences.

    a The flat tail of the . . . helps it to swim well.

    b . . . can see very well at night with their large eyes.

    c The hunter placed . . . to catch wild animals.

    d The Ojibwa was the largest . . . of American Indians.

2 What do you know about American Indians? What do they look like? How do they live? How did they live in the past?

3 Discuss the picture of Grey Owl on the cover. What kind of man was he? What work did he do? When did he live?

4 Read the Introduction to the book. What did Grey Owl want to do?

While you read

5 Circle the right answers.

    a What did Grey Owl wear on stage in 1937?

        i a big hat made of feathers

        ii clothes made of animal skins

        iii modern American clothes

    b What did he show a film of?

        i wild beavers

        ii the trees and lakes of Canada

        iii the people of his tribe

    c What did the people in London think about Canada from Grey Owl's description?

        i It was a difficult and dangerous place.

        ii It was like a wonderful dream.

        iii It was less interesting than the modern world.

    d What was Grey Owl's most important message?

        i The modern way of life was destroying his country.

        ii Indians were not savages.

        iii The modern world was preparing for war.

e Which name for the native people is not used today?

    i Native Americans

    ii Indians

    iii Red Indians

After you read

6 Work in pairs and discuss these questions.

    a Do you agree with Grey Owl's message about the natural world? Why (not)?

    b What opinion did most people have of Native Americans in the 1930s? How did Grey Owl change people's minds?

Pages 5–11

Before you read

7 What do you think Grey Owl's secret was?

While you read

8 Are these sentences right (✓) or wrong (✗)?

    a Grey Owl died while he was traveling to another talk. .....

    b His real name was Archie Belaney. .....

    c He was born in Regina, Canada. .....

    d George Belaney's first business in the U.S. failed. .....

    e George later returned to North America. .....

    f Archie was popular at school. .....

    g Archie loved his first job after school. .....

    h He decided to leave Britain and go to Canada. .....

After you read

9 Discuss these questions.

    a Was Archie a happy child? Why (not)?

    b What kind of man was George Belaney?

    c Was Kittie right to leave Archie with his aunts?

Pages 12–17

Before you read

10 You are going to read about Archie's new life in Canada. How do you think this was different from his early life in England? Make a few notes before you read.

11 Why were these people important to Archie Belaney? Write one-sentence answers.

a Bill Guppy: ....
....

b Michel Mathias and Ned White Bear: ....
....

c The Ojibwa: ....
....

d Angele Egwuna: ....
....

e Angele's uncle: ....
....

f Agnes: ....
....

After you read

12 Discuss these questions.
  a What were the most important things that Archie learned from the Ojibwa? Make a list of five things.
  b Why do you think Archie left Angele and Agnes?

13 Imagine that you are going to Canada. Where will you go? Use the map on pages 14–15 and information from the Internet to plan your trip.

Pages 18–23

Before you read

14 Discuss these questions.
  a The next chapter is called "Wild Days." What do you think Archie did during this time?
  b The First World War started in 1914. What do you think were Archie's feelings about this?

While you read

15 Are these sentences right (✓) or wrong (✗)?
  a To people in Bisco, Archie looked American Indian. .....
  b In Bisco, Archie told lies about his past. .....

    c Marie Girard was a good trapper.   .....

    d Archie worked as a ranger at this time.   .....

    e Archie was in trouble with the Bisco police.   .....

    f He and Marie were married.   .....

    g He was hurt in the war and lost a toe.   .....

    h Archie hated being back in England.   .....

    i Archie married Ivy.   .....

    j Ivy didn't want to move to Canada.   .....

    k Ivy ended the marriage with Archie.   .....

After you read

16 Discuss these questions.

    a How did the First World War change Archie?

    b Why did Archie leave so many women? In your opinion, which was the best for him—Angele, Ivy, or Marie? Why?

Pages 24–31

Before you read

17 Have you ever told an important lie? What was it? What was the result of the lie? How do you feel about it now?

18 In the next part of the book, Archie hears from somebody important from his past. Who do you think this is going to be?

While you read

19 Correct the mistakes in the sentences.

    a Anahareo (Gertrude) grew up in the woods and couldn't read.

    ....

    b She was selling potatoes when Archie first saw her.

    ....

    c Archie loved Anahareo and he moved in with her family.

    ....

    d Archie told Anahareo all of his secrets.

    ....

    e Anahareo loved to go trapping with Grey Owl.

    ....

f Archie's letter to his father was published as a book.

....

g *Country Life* knew that Archie was English.

....

h Archie saved two beavers after he killed their mother.

....

i The government built a cabin for Grey Owl in Edmonton.

....

j Beavers eat fish and use their tails for climbing trees.

....

After you read

20 Discuss these questions.

    a What do you know now about beavers?

    b Why were beavers important to:

       Native Americans?   the first Europeans in Canada?

       Grey Owl?   the Canadian government in the 1930s?

Pages 32–41

Before you read

21 Discuss these questions.

    a Do you think Archie stayed with Anahareo? Why (not)?

    b How did Canadians feel when they discovered the secret of Archie's past?

While you read

22 Answer these questions. Write notes.

    a What was Archie's first book called?

       ....

    b What did he ask people to do at the start of *Tales of an Empty Cabin*?

       ....

    c Which story from this book later became a book?

       ....

    d Why did Anahareo leave?

       ....

e How did the *Nugget* learn Archie's secret?

....

f Which person from his past came to see him in Oxford?

....

After you read

23 Discuss these questions.

    a Which book by Grey Owl would you like to read? Why?

    b In your opinion, did the *Nugget* do the right thing when it didn't tell Archie's secret?

    c What do N. Scott Momaday's words on page 40 mean?

Writing

24 Imagine that you are a person in the book (not Archie). Tell the story of Grey Owl, as you understood it.

25 It is 1937 and Grey Owl is going to give a talk in your London theater. Make a notice to tell people about it.

26 There were a lot of women in Grey Owl's life. What do you think they felt about him? Why?

27 A town in Canada wants to build a place where people can learn about Grey Owl. Write a letter to the local newspaper giving your opinion about this. Is it a good idea? Why (not)?

28 Look again at the picture story on pages 6–11. Tell the story of another part of Archie's life in the same way.

29 Describe an animal or a beautiful area that is in danger in your country. What is the problem? Is there a way of saving it?

30 Write a page for the Internet giving Grey Owl's message to the modern world.

31 Imagine that you can make a new life for yourself. What will you be? Write your story.

WORD LIST

army (n) all the soldiers that fight on land for their country

audience (n) the people who listen to a talk

beaver (n) a North American animal with a wide, flat tail

blow up (v) to destroy something with a sudden, loud noise

cabin (n) a small house made of wood, usually in the forest or in mountains

canoe (n) a long, light, narrow boat that is pointed at both ends

feather (n) one of the light, soft things that covers a bird's body

fur (n) the thick, soft hair that covers the bodies of some animals

hunt (v) to follow animals because you want to kill them

lodge (n) a small house in the country where people usually only stay for a short time; a home that beavers build from wood

native (adj) who were born in that area. Native Americans belong to groups that lived in America before the arrival of Europeans.

nature (n) everything in the world that is not made by people (like weather, animals, and plants)

owl (n) a bird with big eyes and a loud call that looks for its food at night

pony (n) a small horse

publish (v) to print a book or magazine (for example), so people can buy it

ranger (n) someone with the job of looking after forest or other land

savage (n/adj) a very impolite word for someone with a simple way of life. A savage person often attacks people and tries to hurt them.

soul (n) the part of you that, it is believed, continues to exist after your death

trap (n/v) a piece of equipment for catching animals

tribe (n) a group of people, usually with the same language and lifestyle, who live in the same area

Princess Diana
Cherry Gilchrist

Princess Diana, one of the most famous and popular women in the world – the People's Princess.

Read here about Diana's short life, her marriage to Prince Charles, her 'war' with the Royal Family and her love and hard work for sick and poor people all over the world.

Forrest Gump
Winston Groom

Everybody tells Forrest Gump that he's an idiot. But he's a great football player, and he plays the harmonica beautifully. He's also a brave soldier. But can he ever marry the girl he loves? This story of his journey through life is sometimes sad and sometimes very funny.

Dr Jekyll and Mr Hyde
Robert Louis Stevenson

Why is the frightening Mr Hyde a friend of the nice Dr Jekyll? Who is the evil little man? And why does he seem to have power over the doctor? After a terrible murder, everyone is looking for Mr Hyde. But he has disappeared. Or has he?

There are hundreds of Penguin Readers to choose from – world classics, film adaptations, modern-day crime and adventure, short stories, biographies, American classics, non-fiction, plays ...

For a complete list of all Penguin Readers titles, please contact your local Pearson Longman office or visit our website.

Longman Dictionaries

Express yourself with confidence!

Longman has led the way in ELT dictionaries since 1935. We constantly talk to students and teachers around the world to find out what they need from a learner's dictionary.

Why choose a Longman dictionary?

Easy to understand

Longman invented the Defining Vocabulary – 2000 of the most common words which are used to write the definitions in our dictionaries. So Longman definitions are always clear and easy to understand.

Real, natural English

All Longman dictionaries contain natural examples taken from real-life that help explain the meaning of a word and show you how to use it in context.

Avoid common mistakes

Longman dictionaries are written specially for learners, and we make sure that you get all the help you need to avoid common mistakes. We analyse typical learners' mistakes and include notes on how to avoid them.

Innovative CD-ROMs

Longman are leaders in dictionary CD-ROM innovation. Did you know that a dictionary CD-ROM includes features to help improve your pronunciation, help you practice for exams and improve your writing skills?

For details of all Longman dictionaries, and to choose the one that's right for you, visit our website:

www.longman.com/dictionaries